My Guardian Angel

Helper and Friend

By
Rev. Thomas J. Donaghy

Nihil Obstat: James T. O'Connor, S.T.D., Censor Librorum
Imprimatur: ✠ **Patrick J. Sheridan, D.D.**, Vicar General, Archdiocese of New York

The Nihil Obstat and Imprimatur are official declarations that a book or pamphlet is free of doctrinal or moral error. No implication is contained therein that those who have granted the Nihil Obstat and Imprimatur agree with the contents, opinions or statements expressed.

God Made the Angels

God made all things
in heaven and on earth.
The Angels are spirits.
They have no bodies.

When they appear to people on earth,
they are often seen
as people in white robes.

The good Angels love God
and continually praise Him.

They are His faithful servants
and act as His messengers.

Jesus Spoke of the Angels

Jesus spoke of Angels
while He was on earth.

One day, He called a child
and placed him in the midst
of the Apostles.

He told the Apostles
to become like little children.

Then He said:
"Do no harm to one of these little ones.
For their Angels in heaven
always see the Face
of My Father in heaven."

5

Everyone Has a Guardian Angel

Jesus left us the Catholic Church
to lead us to salvation.

The Church has also told us
something about Angels.

Whenever a child is born on earth,
God appoints an Angel
to watch over that child
all the days of his or her life.

These are what we call
the Guardian Angels.

So I have a Guardian Angel,
who is my special Helper and Friend.

In the Morning I Ask My Angel for Help

In heaven,
the greatest joy of the Angels
is to love and serve God.
I want to love God also
and serve Him every day.

Dear Angel-Friend,
help me this day.

Let me think only about things
that are pleasing to God.

Let me speak only about things
that are pleasing to God.

Let me do only things
that are pleasing to God.

10

My Angel Watches Over Me

My Angel is called
a Guardian Angel.

My Angel guards me
and watches over me.

My Angel protects me
from all dangers.

Under my Angel's watchful care,
my body is always safe
and so is my soul.

I should pray often
to my Angel.

My Guardian Angel Teaches Me To Love God's Beautiful World

God made such a beautiful world
for us all.

God made the flowers and trees,
the animals and birds.

God made the sun and sky,
the rivers and seas.

My Angel thanks God each day
for this beautiful world.

My Angel helps me to love
all that God has made.

14

My Angel Helps Me To Love My Family

God loves me
and wants me to be happy.

God gave me my mother and father,
my sisters and brothers.

God wants me to love them
with a special love.

I should ask my Angel
to obtain this gift of God for me.

My Angel will help me
to love my family.

My Angel Helps Me To Be Kind to My Friends

Jesus is happy
when I am kind to others.

My Angel always helps me
to do what pleases Jesus.

If I listen closely, I will hear
the words my Angel whispers in my heart.

They will show me
how I can be kind to my friends everyday.

They will help me
to be good to my playmates.

My Angel Teaches Me To Share

God has given me
a great many blessings.

God has bestowed on me
a home, warm clothing,
good food, and my toys.

Some children have much less
than I have.

My Angel teaches me
to share my gifts with others.

When I share things with others,
I become more pleasing to God.

My Angel Reminds Me To Think about God

The Angels are always
in the presence of God.

They rejoice in thanking
and praising Him.

Children here on earth
are busy all day long.

We play, read, or watch television.
Sometimes we forget God.

My Angel reminds me
to stop at times
and to think about God.

My Angel Helps Me To Pray

My Angel prays to God
for me.

My Angel also helps me
to pray.

Who could teach me
how to pray
better than an Angel!

These heavenly spirits were created
to love and praise God.

They know how to pray.

My Angel Helps Me To Obey My Parents

I know
my parents love me very much.

They want only what is best
for me.

When I obey them,
I will be happy.

My Angel helps me
to obey them in everything.

When I do so,
I honor them and make them happy.

My Angel Helps Me
To Please Jesus

Children who obey God
please Jesus very much.

They are His special friends
and are filled with His gifts.

They even become like Jesus
in some ways.

My Angel helps me
to obey God each day.

This will please God
and keep me close to Jesus.

My Angel Watches Over Me While I Sleep

When my busy day is over,
I'm tired and ready for sleep.

But my Angel is not tired
and needs no sleep.

My Angel stands by me
and watches over my sleep.

With my Angel near me
I feel safe and sound.

How blest am I
to have an Angel
of my very own!

30

I Love My Guardian Angel

Dear Lord,
I thank You for making the Angels.

I also thank You
for giving me my Angel-Friend.

And I love you,
my Angel-Friend.

I thank you
for alway being there for me.

Stay with me today
and always.

Prayer to My Guardian Angel

Angel of God,
my Guardian dear,
God' s love for me
has sent you here.

Ever this day
be at my side,
to light and guard,
to rule and guide.

MAGNIFICENT EDITIONS THAT BELONG IN
EVERY CATHOLIC HOME

FIRST MASS BOOK—Ideal Children's Mass Book with all the official Mass prayers. Colored illustrations of the Mass and the Life of Christ. Confession and Communion Prayers. **Ask for No. 808**

PICTURE BOOK OF SAINTS—By Rev. L. Lovasik, S.V.D. Illustrated Lives of the Saints in full color for Young and Old. It clearly depicts the lives of over 100 popular Saints in word and picture. **Ask for No. 235**

MY FIRST PRAYERBOOK—By Rev. Lawrence G. Lovasik, S.V.D. Beautiful new prayerbook that provides prayers for the main occasions in a child's life. Features simple language, easy-to-read type, and full-color illustrations. **Ask for No. 205**

THE MASS FOR CHILDREN—By Rev. Jude Winkler, OFM Conv. New beautifully illustrated Mass Book that explains the Mass to children and contains the Mass responses they should know. It is sure to help children know and love the Mass. **Ask for No. 215**

LIVES OF THE SAINTS—New Revised Edition. Short life of a Saint and prayer for every day of the year. Over 50 illustrations. Ideal for daily meditation and private study. **Ask for No. 870**

CATHOLIC PICTURE BIBLE—By Rev. L. Lovasik, S.V.D. Thrilling, inspiring and educational for all ages. Over 110 Bible stories retold in simple words, and illustrated in full color. **Ask for No. 435**

St. Joseph FIRST CHILDREN'S BIBLE—By Father Lovasik, S.V.D. Over 50 of the best-loved stories of the Bible retold for children. Each story is written in clear and simple language and illustrated by an attractive and superbly inspiring illustration. A perfect book for introducing very young children to the Bible. **Ask for No. 135**

The STORY OF JESUS—By Father Lovasik, S.V.D. A large-format book with magnificent full colored pictures for young readers to enjoy and learn about the life of Jesus. Each story is told in simple and direct words. **Ask for No. 535**

WHEREVER CATHOLIC BOOKS ARE SOLD